THE TREE OF SALVATION

For information address:

J2B Publishing LLC
4251 Columbia Part Road
Pomfert, MD 20675
www.J2BLLC.com
GladToDoIt@gmail.com

Cover Photo: Picture of a wooden Christian cross on St. Cuthbert's Isle, Holy Island, Northumberland.
Title Page Photo: Ian Britton, June 4, 2008, Flikr.com:

Printed and bound in the United States of America

ISBN: 978-1-948747-60-8

THE TREE OF SALVATION

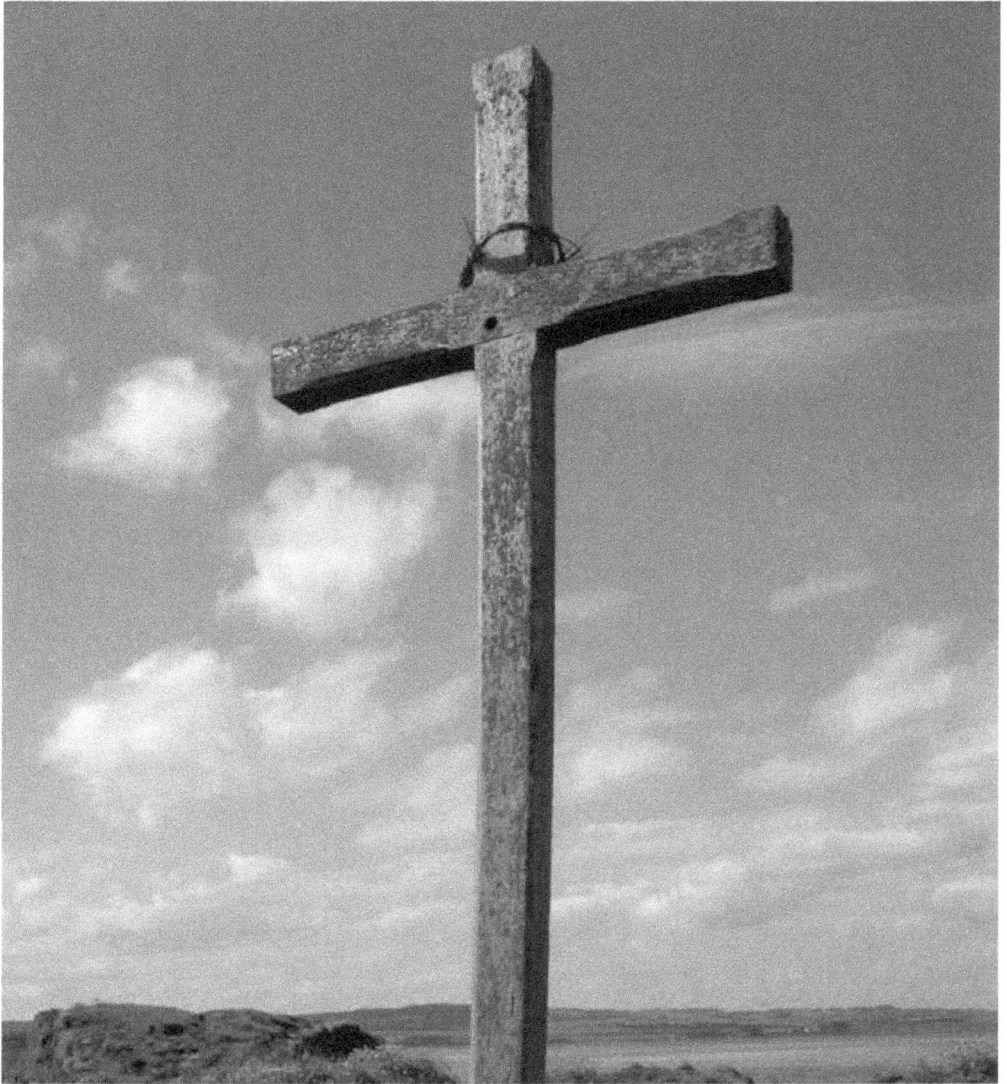

Richard I. Gold

J2B Publishing

Also by Richard I. Gold

God's Agenda: Religious Poems Vol. I
Mary's Lamb and other Christmas Poems
God's Love - Easter Poems
Sayings for the Believer
Work is a 4-Letter Word
Free Advice
Life is a Trip
Christmas Trees and Mistletoe
Cost of the Cross

DEDICATION

My thanks for the support from my wife, Penelope Gold, and to those who have reviewed these poems and made valuable suggestions.

CONTENTS

INTRODUCTION

For the Christian, the origin of our opportunity to be made right with God, for now and forever was sealed when He sent His Son to be a Witness for Him. The climax of God's love was when Jesus hung on the cross. Then, by His power God raised Him from the grave on the third day.

When Jesus died, to his followers this seemed the end. In truth it was the end of the beginning because it brought about the most profound revolution in our relationship with God and with other people.

ON A TREE HE DIED FOR US

On a tree He died for us
Raised to life again so we can trust

Raised by God on high
Raised so our soul can draw nigh

We must trust, live and obey
Our sin debt He did pay

Praise His Holy Name
For the evil, He came to tame

Glory to our Father above
Gave His Son to us in love

Glory to the One who died
Glory to the Holy One crucified

Glory to the One our souls He knew
Glory to His teachings true

We must worship in His Way
He came our sin debt to pay

Now He lives in Heaven on high
So that to God we may draw nigh

HIS HOLY WAY, AMEN

His Holy Way we must go
Amen, amen

Seeds of salvation He did sow
Amen, amen

All glory to His presence here
Amen, amen

When we need Him, He is near
Amen, amen

Love Him more than our self
Amen, amen

Love Him more than our wealth
Amen, amen

FORGIVENESS

God loved mankind so much
He sent His only Son
To teach us how to live
To die when the beginning was begun

We suffer many wrongs
That others to us have done
How can we forgive?
How can forgiveness be begun?

But our sins against God
Are much, much the greater
If He can forgive us at all
It is because He is our maker

"Forgive them" were the words of Christ
As He hung upon the tree
If He could forgive His tormentors
Surely I can forgive thee

THERE IS ONE WAY FOR SALVATION

There is one Way for salvation
There is one Way to God above
That Way is Jesus Christ
For God is a God of love

We depend upon Him
Each and every day
To give us what we need
To hear us when we pray

We can only love our God
Love Him with all our heart
So that in eternity
From Him we shall never depart

GOD'S ONE WAY

There is One Way to God
And only one
It is the Holy One
It is God's Holy Son

Begotten of God
Lived among men
Has seen us from the first
Will see us at the end

Follow the Way
To a holy life
All other ways
Will lead to eternal strife

We can know the Way
The only Way given among men
By which we must be saved
A new life to begin

It is by the death of Christ
Who came to show us the Way
How to live our life
He hears us when we pray

Christ was raised from the grave
Raised by the hand of God
From death to life everlasting
For us ever we're beneath the sod

PRAISE THE LORD

Praise the Lord
Praise His Holy Name
He who sent His Holy Son
From age to age the same

Offers us salvation
By belief in His only Son
Will guide us in His Way
Till life's battles are won

We can only follow in His steps
To learn what we must do
To find God's will for us
That is just and faithful and true

SOME BELIEVE

Some believe to cheat is wrong
Some believe that it is all right
Some believe that what we do
Is governed by our own insight

We follow what we know
What is within our mind?
Be it either bad or good
Either cruel or kind

Does it matter what a man believes
Or yet a woman too
It does not change the facts
But changes what we do

COME TO GOD, COME TO TRUTH

To come to God is to come to truth
So eternal life we will have won
For God has shown The Way
Through Jesus Christ, His Son

Though we cannot know the mind of God
His will we must seek
So that as through life we go
His holy words we can speak

There are many things
That in the world do tempt
To be a saint of God
Does not make us exempt

Live by the Word of God
God has shown the Way
So we may be one with God
Through all the world's fray

Although we can never perfect be
In this world of toil and sin
We must forever try
So we can heaven win

But God has shown the Way
Has shown us how to live
To be one of God's people
His Word he does give

TO WORSHIP THE LORD

I'll go to church to worship the Lord
To be with the people who pray
To hear some holy words of love
On how to live my life each day

The world has many lures
To lead my feet astray
But being in a place of worship
Keeps me on His Holy Way

There is but one way to God
To be pleasing is what He does demand
It is through His Holy Son
The teachings of the Son of Man

I know not what tomorrow brings
Whether bad or good
But by The Way of God
I'll do what I know I should

THE LORD IS MY SHEPHERD

The Lord is my shepherd
The Lord is my king
By His hand and by His love
I shall not need anything

When I walk through darkness
He is my Holy Light
He keeps my soul
In the darkest night

There is no other one
Who knows my all
He will sustain me
Whenever I face a fall

But there is the Way of God
Who has sent His Son
To show us His Holy Way
Whenever our life is done

So let us follow in His Way
Though life's trials begin
To do what we should
His truth keeps us from all sin

This is the will of God
This is His Holy Way
So that in the end of life
Our sin debt Jesus did pay

Remember the time long ago
What was given to men
A Way to have eternal life
We may all continue to begin

GOD IS LOVE

Whenever we go out
With a message from God above
The message we must carry
"God is love"

We cannot speak about other things
Which life does bring
When under the influence of God
This is what the angels sing

So let us know the will of God
For He sent His Holy Son
With salvation for every person
May be accepted, eternal life begun

But let the truth not stand alone
There is none else to have
But to all people on earth
This is the truth we must give

SALVATION IS THE GIFT OF GOD

Salvation is the gift of God
To those whom He choose to give
Man's quest for grace
Determines how we live

We worship what we do not truly know
The face of God we cannot see
But by His power and by His grace
We will with Him forever be

So pray to God with all your heart
Love Him with mind and body and soul
For if we find grace in His sight
His power will make us whole

TO KNOW GOD

The world is filled with many things
Some things we can know
We learn about most of these
As through life we go

There are other things
Beyond what we can comprehend
Of which we can never learn
If we did, wrong on us would descend

There are things beyond our knowledge
Beyond the understanding of men
That we cannot know in this life
As numerous as beach's sand

We cannot see the face of God
We cannot know His awesome power
Above the history of all men
His presence doth tower

We can know some of His will
For it is what desires He
How to worship Him
His holiness our mind's eye to see

It is by His will we help
Those with less than we have
The widows and the orphans
To the destitute we should give

Although we cannot see God's face
Although no whisper in our ear
We can know the will of God
Worship Him in reverence and in fear

It is by His Holy Word
That the nature of God shines through
Learn what the Word does say
For it is good and just and true

THE GRACE OF GOD

In life we do bad and good
With punishment and reward
Here on earth, we struggle
To hit a Holy Chord

But the Eternal Judge
Who has for us a standard set
We can be very sure
What we give, we will get

But if we can be forgiven
For the evil we do
It is by the grace of God
That we can make our soul true

There is no other way
Than Jesus Christ, God's Son
As we bow below the Heavenly Throne
When life's race is run

THERE IS ONLY ONE GOD IN HEAVEN

There is only one God in Heaven
There is room for only one
Who so loved the world
He sent us His only Son

The Son is the Father
The Father is the Son
By the Son's teachings
The two are made one

We cannot understand
The dimensions of the mind
But the humble man may worship
And salvation find

One in three
Three in one
The Father, the Son and the Holy Spirit
The three are one

This is a great mystery
There are things we can never know
But of this, by grace
By the three our spirit will grow

IT'S HARD TO BE HOLY

It's hard to be holy
In this unholy world
When faced with temptations
That makes our toes curl

Temptations for wealth
For love and for fame
Will sear our soul
Will blacken our name

It takes a saint
Temptations to overcome
For me, when faced with temptation
It's best if I run

For sin is not in temptation
Nor yet in a passing thought
But sin is in the doing
In what evil it wrought

We must guard ourselves
Guard forever our mind
Because in the dwelling upon
Will evil our life find

So discipline our mind
Know the right Way
Guard our every action
Be careful what we say

What we say affects others
They think our actions are so
But the quality of our soul
Is something they can never know

No man is a holy god
Our will can never be
We must follow our God
If it is heaven we would see

BELIEVERS CAN BE GOD'S CHILDREN

Believers can be God's children
The Bible tells us so
If we His commandments keep
His Holy Love we will know

God's children have privileges
To finally live with God
But while here on earth
His Holy Path we must trod

The power to be God's children
Is really an awesome task
No amount of good living
Can our evil mask

But through the name of Jesus
We receive from God
That we may live with Him
When our body is beneath the sod

WALK THE STRAIGHT AND NARROW

Walk the straight and narrow
The path the saints have trod
For in following this Holy Path
You find the will of God

The path of life
The holy path to heaven lead
For the mercy of God
Will give us the salvation that we plead

There is no other way
Given to the children of men
To insure that it will be heaven
When our life shall end

BY HIS TEACHINGS

By His teachings
We have the Way to live
By His death
We are saved from destruction
By His resurrection
We will live in eternity

By following His teachings
We can live right
By His death
We can be justified before God
By His resurrection
We can have eternal life

By God's will
He lived
By God's sacrifice
He died
By God's power
He was raised to life again

WE ARE JUSTIFIED

Within our mind
What we believe, we believe is true
But when we face the facts
We would know what heaven knew

We're always justified
To ourselves in all we do
But eternal justification
Comes from doing what to God is true

So we must live as we are taught
By the only Son of God
If we would be made right with God
Heaven's gate we would see

WOULD YOU BE RIGHT WITH GOD?

Would you be right with God?
When you lay beneath the sod
Would you be right with God?
When you die, receive His nod

What you do must be with Him right
So that when you work with all your might
The product of your hand and mind
Will be judged kind

Then love others
Love those of God
Work for the right
Give all good the nod

AND KNOW

To be saved
It is by God's grace
By being saved
You shall see His face

JESUS' NAME

Whenever we pray to God
We ask for what we will
But God, in His good grace
Gives to us whatever He will

Jesus said to ask in His name
And he will give what we ask
But we need to be very sure
That when we ask, we are in His will

For to ask in Jesus' Name
Is to ask in the power of Who He is
To know what we must believe and do
To have our souls aligned with his

So ask in Jesus' name
But be very sure
That the glory that is given
Is to God endure

BY THE POWER OF GOD

By the power of God
The world was created

By the will of God
Mankind was given life

By the judgement of God
Man was given free will

By the love of God
God sent his only Son

By the grace of God
God gave us the Way

By the eternal existence of God
We are given the Way to eternal life

By the judgement of God
All mankind will be given justice

By the power of His Son
We can be justified

By the life of God's Son
We can find the Holy Way

By the teachings of God's Son
We can find the Way to live

CHRISTIANS MUST BE DIFFERENT

If we are Christians
Called by the name of Christ
We must be different from the world
This is the price

For if Christians are not different
In this world of toil and sin
What it means to follow Christ
The world will never comprehend

It is not easy
To follow our Lord
But the goal of our living
Is to have the spirit's sword

For the wiles of this world
Will ensnare us as we rest
Lead us the wrong way
If we do not stand the test

The test of the spirit
Comes from the pleasure of sin
Pulling on our passion's desire
Telling us to begin

So the Christian must remember
Whose we are
And let our desire depart
The way we walk in life's evil bar

THE LOVE OF GOD IS STRONG

The love of God is strong
Reaching from heaven above
To earth's poor child
To all human kind with love

The wrath of God is terrible
Best not go there
For in the cleansing of the soul
There is only fear

The justice of God is holy
Judging all we do
If we cross the line
The results will be untrue

For God has given us the Way
To live as we should
When we are to be judged
We will wish we could

But our life on earth
Is but a fleeting time
In this world of woe
It is our need to do our best

That God may bless our soul
As through the world we go
That the peace of God
May be the way we know

WHEN IS THE TIME TO WORSHIP GOD

When is the time to worship God?
Morning, noon or night
We go to God in prayer
To seek His Holy Light

When is the time to pray?
The past, the future or now
To seek God's Holy Guidance
To learn His Holy How

Any time is the time to worship God
Any time is the time to pray
Carry His Holy Presence
Through both night and day

COME TO THE LIGHT

Come, come, come to the Light
Leave the darkness behind
The light will dispel all evil
Will clear the clouded mind

Let no one stop you
Let no one despair
For the joy of living
Will be with you there

No one can fully see
No one can understand
The message the Light gives
The love within its hand

Rewards for those who do right
Love, justice from the Lord
Follow His Holy Example
Live by His Holy Word

SPIRIT OF THE LIVING GOD

Spirit of the living God
Father, Spirit and Son
To you is the victory
The many battles won

Come down to us, we pray
Teach us what we must to do
That to Your Holy Will
We must forever be true

Where is His path for us?
The Way that we must trod
It is the path of life
That leads to the feet of God

YOU'RE NOT A NOBODY

"You're not a nobody
You're a Child of God"
So the church sign read
From now till you're beneath the sod

The Bible calls you a child
An heir to the Holy Throne
A leader without doubt
One whose good deeds are known

Before you inherit the throne
You must face your cross
For what in this life is gain
May turn into eternal loss

If you have faith
You are the Heavenly Father's Child
You will stand before His face
And see is His Holy smile

FAITH

We come to a fork in the road of life
We can go either left or right
We make a choice based upon hope
Walk along with all our might

It is by faith Christians walk
Along the path of life
Through the world of love and hate
Through this place of strife

Faith is the golden assurance
Faith and hope and love
That when we cross the great divide
We will have a home above

THE CHRISTIAN LIFE

In this world of toil and sin
The Christian life doth shine
It is a beacon to God
The devil to bind

The power God does have
Is greater than we can know
It is in the power of love
That in our lives does grow

The Christian life is given to God
To follow in His Way
So that we may forever live
As we do whatever He doth say

The Christian life is more than that
For we can become a Child of God
So that we may forever live with Him
When our body lies beneath the sod

TRUTH OF JESUS CHRIST

We live in this world of toil and sin
Not knowing the truth we should
That belongs to our gracious Lord
It is not what the mind of man would

For the end of it all
The battles lost and won
Are in the hand of God
Who sent His only Son

We can but trust the message
Sent through Christ to us
On how to live and how to die
How to eternally trust

GOD'S AGAPE

To what shall we liken the love of God?
It is more than we can know
So rare and so holy in every way
It saves us from every woe

Would that men could love
As the Way of God
But only One has ever been
To save us from the sod

The only Way we may know
The mind of the Holy One
Is to love in word and deed
To follow His Holy Son

For if we live a thousand years
A thousand years and a day
We will never be able
Our soul's sin debt to pay

For though we live in a world of sin
Immersed in it our whole being is
By the death of the Holy Son
God will let us be forever His

Our sins may be washed away
By the agape love
That can only be ours
From the One above

There is nothing we can do
To deserve the love of the Most High
But by His love and by His Son
To His Throne we may draw nigh

WE ARE GOD'S

God can use all of us
Whatever we may know
To do His good will
To make His will so

We cannot disrupt the will of God
It moves like a mighty hand
Along the corridors of history
Throughout the wide land

So what must we do?
To serve the will of God
We should strive to act this way
To bend to His Holy Rod

FAITH IN THE FUTURE

The future we cannot see
It is a blank slate
But it will get here
All we have to do is wait

But there are things we wish
Things not now
It is this faith in the future
That we will know how

The faith in the future
Is the hope we have
But what it will really be
Is what chance will give

If we do not have a goal
A place for which we hope
When the future gets here
We will not be able to cope

It is by the faith we live
That what tomorrow brings
Will be what we want
Our future, our things

HOPE

We live in a world
A world where things go bad
If this is all there is
Our future would look sad

We should not let it get us down
For today is not forever
Things will improve
Although it may seem never

It is this brighter future
Not the present dope
For it is God's eternal grace
On which we place our hope

SAVED FROM THE FALL

Jesus was born in a distant land
Born mankind to call
Born to teach us how to live
Born to save us from the fall

That which caused the fall of mankind
Is still at work
We try to do the best
In our life it does lurk

As time goes by and men live and die
I do not know the cause of hate
But I am sure that at the end
Will be found at Hell's gate

But God so loved mankind
Why I can never tell
As we walk the path of life
His love shall never fail

God looks from heaven above
God finds us in all things
Worthy of His care and love
As before His Throne we bring

THE THREE

There are mysteries we can never know
We wonder how it can be
That our Holy God
Is one, yet three

God is the Father of all
His love is greater than we can know
By His will and by His might
He made the world so

God is the Son on earth
Who came to save us all
That we can from our faults
Be saved from the eternal fall

God is the Holy Spirit within
The power of God in His church
That we may not know defeat
When we care for His people much

Three in one
One in three
We do not understand
But it is salvation for you, for me

MANY DID NOT KNOW MY JESUS

Many did not know my Jesus
Many do not know Him now
They try to live a good life
But they have no idea how

There are commands, ten
All men must keep
But when they live their lives
What they sow they did not want to reap

But Jesus taught the truth
Jesus is the only Way
That will lead to heaven
As we live from day to day

WE ARE HERE TO WORSHIP GOD

We are here to worship God
We are here to worship our Lord
We are here to worship God
Praise the Lord

We have come to praise God
We have come to praise our Lord
We have come to praise God
Praise our God

I will sing praises to God
I will sing praises to my Lord
I will sing praises to God
Worship my Lord

CHILDREN ARE A GIFT FROM GOD

Children are a gift from God
A continuation of our own
We must give them what they need
And make for them a home

Children are to be loved and held
To be treated most tenderly
For when they grow
They will know
That we gave them love

As into the world they go
They carry what we have given them
Pass it on to their children
Whenever they have their own

So do not squander your time
That you can instruct and guide
It is for the future that you are preparing
In your hands and time it does reside

PRAISE THE LORD

Praise the Lord
Praise His Holy Name
From age to age
His will is the same

Praise the Lord
Praise His Holy place
Though mortal man may never know
The glory of His grace

Praise the Lord
Praise him in all the earth
He sent His only Son
To give mankind the second birth

Praise the Lord
Praise Him for Who He is
He created and cares for us
His will makes us His

Praise the Lord
Much we can never know
For by His love and by His power
His purpose makes it so

RELIGION IS THE WAY OF LIFE

Religion is the Way of life
It permeates your very soul
But if you only talk it
Its precepts get very old

But if it is a part of you
So that you follow on
Your life will show your soul
If you take it home

Lip service is fine
For you must talk the talk
But if it is truly yours
You must walk the walk

BIG ANGELS, LITTLE ANGELS

Big angels come and stay
A part of my life
I found my own angel
Now she is my wife

Little angels come and go
Come when little they are
Grow up so very fast
Leave when they get a car

Love your little angels while they're yours
Let them know they're loved
For when they go off on their own
They're gone for good

THE RIVER OF LIFE

The river of life
Runs through time and space
It started as a trickle
With itself made a place

The river of life
Carries all along
We cannot fight it
Its flow is too strong

When we come to the ocean
That is the end, the sea
The ship of heaven
Will be waiting for you and me

GLORY, GLORY, GLORY

Glory, glory, glory
Praise Him, praise Him
Praise Him all beings
Glorify His name
Glorify His name
Glorify His name all ye people

Sing His praises, sing His praises
Sing His praises all beings great and small
For God has done a mighty thing
He sent His only Son
To show us how to live
To show us the way of salvation

Praise Him
Praise Him
Praise Him with all your being
Praise Him with all your soul
Praise Him with all your earnings
Praise Him for all His works

For God is truly love
For God is truly love
For God is love that we should live
Should live with Him above

CHRISTIAN BAPTISM

For the Christian, Baptism
Is a contract with God
To live according to His teachings
Until we're beneath the sod

Baptism is of water
Of spirit and Christ's blood
It is to know the Word
That Christian understood

Commitment is a personal thing
Only we, our self can make
For in the world at large
Temptations will our attention take

So comment to the will of God
Make this your joy
Love God with all you have
For God is the universe's Roy

THE BLESSED ONES

The blessed ones keep away from evil
They do not help others to sin
They keep from those who scoff
They keep the right to the end

The blessed ones love the Lord
They are thankful day and night
They are sturdy as the evergreen
Their fruit is of the right

Those who love the Lord
Those who worship through His Son
Will prosper in all they do
Will in the end have won

The wicked are different
They have no anchor in life
They cannot stand the judgment
Their life is full of strife

So walk in the Way of the righteous
For this Way will forever be
For God knows the way of the righteous
His Will they will forever see

The way of the sinner is different
It is a way that will not last
For the wicked will parish
Their day of glory will pass

So, know the will of God in all life
Study to show that you truly know
For as you live on earth
Your actions and life will surely show

A MESSAGE FROM ABOVE

Within the time of life
There comes a message from above
To all who live upon the earth
"God is love"

We can but know what is to know
As given from the Holy Hand
It is the will of the Most High
To the children of men

If God did not love our kin
Did not really care
Then we would pay the price
For all the evil there

But God does care with love
That we may know His Holy Will
To do what is right and good
Be forgiven for our ill

MY LAST DAY

Soon I will be going
My soul will leave this earth
I've had a long and good life
From when my mother gave me birth

I hope I will be missed
By those for whom I care and love
But do not grieve for me
My soul will be with God above

I've done many things
Had memories both bad and good
Sorry for some things I've done
Wished I had done others when I could

But soon I will leave this world of pain
My body will be beneath the sod
The memories of this world left behind
Will be the providence of God

I'll be on a new and holy journey
To the land beyond earth's sod
That by the grace of His Holy Son
I'll see the face of God

CHILD OF MAN

Child of man
Son of God
We are born to sorrow
Till we're beneath the sod

Worship the Lord
Maker of man
For worship is due
From those who can

The way of the world
Is not from heaven on high
So with humble adoration
To God's Throne draw nigh

RISE UP

Rise up
Rise up oh one of God
Rise up and sing His praise
For by His hand
For by His love
We are sustained all our days

Rise up
Rise up and serve our God
Our opportunity to do good
Till we're beneath the cold dark sod

Rise up
Rise up and do our best
So that when before God's judgment seat
We will have stood the test

FROM THE PIT OF DESPAIR

From the pit of despair
My soul looks up to Thee
God, where is your salvation
That'll set me free

The chains that bind me
The despair that enfolds me
Are more than I can handle
My only hope is in Thee

I praise you for your salvation
That comes through your Son
From my pit of despair
Your victory can be won

Hope of the future
Salvation from God
So we may live forever
When our body is beneath the sod

HOW PEACEFUL IS THE RIVER

How peaceful is the river
That runs through our life
It leads us to the land of peace
Away from the day of strife

Let us follow that river
As far as it may go
So that at the end of it all
Eternal peace we may know

There is a land of peace and rest
Where we may forever be
That when our Lord comes for us
His glorious face we may see

THE MESSAGE IN THE BIBLE

The message in the Bible
To the children of men
Is one we must learn
We must study it again and again

The message is one
For this is the fact
From what you are doing
Clean up your act

You live a long life
You look for the truth
If you would know this
You best learn it in your youth

THE WORDS ON THE WALL

The words on the wall
Can great wisdom contain
But wisdom is in the application
Not abstract in the main

Once a king of Persia
His wise men did call
"Give me a saying true for all times
One I can put on the wall"

After many a day
The wise men returned in the Way
"This, Oh king, is the saying
'This too, shall pass away'"

A BLESSING

A Scottish Blessing

From ghostiest and Ghoulies
And things that go kabaptity in the night
The good Lord save us

Updated version

From druggies and terrorist
And things that go boom in the night
The good Lord save us

ABOUT THE AUTHOR

Richard Gold was born in Bartow, Florida and attended college and worked for the Government for 40 years. He has been a Christian and writing poems for as long. Gold is now retired giving him time to continue writing. Gold lives in Indian Head, Maryland with Penny, his artistically talented wife.